Garry Chambers and Alan Wightman are two of Britain's most prolific TV comedy writers, not to mention Britain's two most prolific lightbulb changers.

Garry Chambers and
Alan Wightman

Futura

How many sheep does it take to change a lightbulb?

One ... two ... three ... four ... five zzzzzzzz.

Do you know how many ex-Mr Elizabeth Taylors it takes to change a lightbulb?

I do! I do! I do! I do! I do! I do!

How many Richard Bransons does it take to change a lightbulb?

Three. One to announce in a blaze of publicity that he'll do it. One to balls it up. And one to stick the taxpayer with the bill.

How many Michael Caines does it take to change a lightbulb?

Not many people know that ... including me.

What number of Patrick McGoohans does it take to change a lightbulb?

'I am not a number, I am a free man!'

How many Irishmen does it take to change a lightbulb?

'Would you mind putting the light on, Sean, it's so dark in here I can't find the socket.'

How many Ted Rogers's does it take to change a lightbulb?

I wouldn't let him change it if I were you. Ted's all fingers and thumbs.

What sound is made when an incontinent person drops a lightbulb?

A little tinkle.

Can a Red Indian change a lightbulb?

How?

Only one.

How many mind readers does it take to change a lightbulb?

How many procrastinators does it take to change a lightbulb?

I'll tell you tomorrow … or the day after.

How many Richard Nixons does it take to change a lightbulb?

One. But as he does it he says, 'I am not a lightbulb changer.'

Why shouldn't you ask Marti Webb and Wayne Sleep to change a lightbulb?

Because they'll make a song and dance about it.

How many surrealists does it take to change a lightbulb?

The fish.

How does Gerald Ford change a lightbulb?

Well, first he picks himself up off the floor …

How many electrician's daughters does it take to change a lightbulb?

She was only an electrician's daughter but she knew what's watt.

How many Selina Scotts does it take to change a lightbulb?

Two. One to change it and one to ask inane questions like – how many Selina Scotts does it take to change a lightbulb?

How many SAS members does it take to change a lightbulb?

Ten. One to change it and nine to surround it and yell at the old bulb to give itself up.

How many Quasimodos does it take to change a lightbulb?

Just the one if he's played by Charles Light-On.

How many pantomime dames does it take to change a lightbulb?

Two.

'Oh no it doesn't!'

How does Ronnie Corbett change a lightbulb?

First, he borrows the ladder from his budgie …

How many Air Raid Wardens does it take to change a lightbulb?

'Put that ruddy light out!'

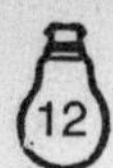

How many Lionel Blairs does it take to change a lightbulb?

Two. One to change it and one to hog the limelight of it.

How many Cyril Smiths does it take to change a lightbulb?

There's nothing light about Cyril.

How many Shirley MacLaines does it take to change a lightbulb?

In previous lives the bulb was a hammer, a doorknob, a razor, a stirrup and a shoehorn.

How many gullible paperback book buyers does it take to change a lightbulb?

The answer is on page 436.

How many Orson Welles's does it take to change a lightbulb?

Before the old bulb died it said, 'Rosebud'.

How many Ken Livingstones does it take to change a lightbulb?

Two. One to change it and one to claim the old bulb was assassinated by M.I.5.

How many punk rockers does it take to change a lightbulb?

'Bollocks!'

How many Bobby Ewings does it take to change a lightbulb?

No need to change it. The dead bulb just came back to life in the shower.

How many model girls does it take to change a lightbulb?

Five. One to do it and four to say, 'I could do that.'

How many Bob Geldofs does it take to change a lightbulb?

'For Christ's sake, how many more light-bulbs have to die before people wake up and take notice?'

How many Sooties does it take to change a lightbulb?

Just the one, but Harry Corbett will have a hand in it.

How many Cockney taxi drivers does it take to change a lightbulb?

'What? Go all the way up that ladder and come back empty? Not bloody likely, guv!'

How many Bernie Winters's does it take to change a lightbulb?

One. But Schnorbitz must be there to read him the instructions.

How many Ringo Starrs does it take to change a lightbulb?

None. A session lightbulb changer will do it.

How many *Sun* readers does it take to change a lightbulb?

Like everything else, the lightbulb is over their heads.

How many Ferdinand Marcos's does it take to change a lightbulb?

Ten. They'll hold a ballot on who should do it and Ferdinand will win by 675 votes to 9.

How many Two Ronnies's does it take to change a lightbulb?

'So it's a good light from me.'

'And it's a good light from him.'

How many Dirty Harrys does it take to change a lightbulb?

'I know what you're thinking. You're thinking did he change six lightbulbs or only five? Well, in all this excitement I forgot to count. But seeing as this is a Philips Prismatic SL18, the most powerful lightbulb in the world and liable to light your entire head up, the question you must be asking yourself is do you feel lucky? Well, do you, punk?'

How many Koo Starks does it take to change a lightbulb?

Three. One to change it. One to refuse to talk to the press about it. And one to use the experience as an excuse to promote her latest exhibition of crappy snapshots.

How does the Walt Disney Studio change a lightbulb?

They don't. They just revive the original every seven years.

How does Burt Reynolds change a lightbulb?

What do *you* care? You never go to his movies anymore.

How does Michael Barrymore change a lightbulb?

Exactly the same way John Cleese does.

How does Dolly Parton change a lightbulb?

I'm not sure. I think I'll sit here and watch her.

How many dry cleaners does it take to change a lightbulb?

'I'm sorry, sir, the bulb must have faded. But you did leave it here at your own risk.'

How many newsreaders does it take to change a lightbulb?

Probably five or six. Well, it takes *two* of them just to read the headlines these days.

Why does a priest take so long to change a lightbulb?

He spends so much time giving the old one the last rites.

How many Joan Rivers's does it take to change a lightbulb?

Two. One to change it and one to turn the situation into a joke about her gynaecologist.

Why does Michael Jackson burst into tears when a lightbulb blows?

He thinks Tinkerbell died.

What does an insurance salesman say when a lightbulb blows?

'You never know when these things are going to happen.'

How does Bob Monkhouse change a lightbulb?

Perfectly.

How does Bill Wyman change a lightbulb?

He gets a girl a quarter his age to do it and then claims nothing happened.

How many Des O'Connor fans does it take to change a lightbulb?

Both of them.

How many Speedy Gonzalez's does it take … too late, he's already done it.

What *doesn't* Sean Penn say when he changes a lightbulb?

'Cheese.'

How many Barry Manilow fans does it take to change a lightbulb?

None. They've all got their candles lit.

How does Derek Jameson change a lightbulb?

That's an easy question. The really difficult one to answer is – how did he get his own radio show?

How does Bet Lynch change a lightbulb?

Easy. She just unscrews one of the spare ones hanging from her ears.

What does Andrew Lloyd Webber do when his lightbulb blows?

Moves to a bigger house.

How many Quincys does it take to change a lightbulb?

Just the one, but he's busy right now performing an autopsy on the dead bulb.

How many New Yorkers does it take to change a lightbulb?

Forget it, they don't want to get involved.

How many Hare Krishna followers does it take to change a lightbulb?

None. They're already enlightened.

How many video shop assistants does it take to change a lightbulb?

'Aw ... if only you'd asked earlier, sir. Someone's just been in for it. Shall I order you a copy?'

How does Robert De Niro change a lightbulb?

Well, first he puts on 200 lbs and grows a beard ...

Who's going to film Sting when he changes a lightbulb?

Only an idiot. Every film he's been in has died at the box-office.

How long does it take Bruce Springsteen to change a lightbulb?

Four hours ... but that doesn't include the encores.

How many boy scouts does it take to change a lightbulb?

Two. One to change it and one to tie knots in the flex.

How many Greenham Common women does it take to change a lightbulb?

'You sexist pig! We've got more important things to do than change lightbulbs!'

How many dentists does it take to change a lightbulb?

Three. One to take the old one out. One to put the new one in. And one to empty your wallet while you're in the chair.

Why do lightbulbs blow when Bruce Willis is in the room?

He's very difficult to work with.

How long does it take Max Wall to change a lightbulb?

Half an hour. Five minutes to change it and twenty-five to do his funny walk.

How do they change lightbulbs over on Elm Street?

In their sleep.

When does Gary Glitter change a lightbulb?

In between comebacks.

How many Lloyd Grossmans does it take to change a lightbulb?

Two. One to change it and one to criticize the style of the bulb.

How does Richard Gere change a lightbulb?

First he has to take his shirt off …

How many SAS men does it take to change a lightbulb?

One. And you'll never know he's done it.

How many Michael Nicholsons of ITN does it take to change a lightbulb?

Two. One to change it and one to pronounce it as 'bightlulb'.

How many Johnny Carsons does it take to change a lightbulb?

Sorry, John, your ex-wife got custody of all the electrical fittings too.

How many Ex-Lax testers does it take to change a lightbulb?

'Sorry … must dash!'

Samantha Fox, can you change a lightbulb?

'Nah, mate, I don't do that sort of fing no more. I'm a singer now.'

How many gays does it take to change a lightbulb?

Three. One to do it and two to talk about him while he's out of the room.

How does Freddie Starr change a lightbulb?

First he eats the old one …

How many alternative comedians does it take to change a lightbulb?

We'll never know. They refused to appear in a gagbook.

How does Cilla Black change a lightbulb?

With her mouth shut … please God!

How many 'soap' stars does it take to change a lightbulb?

Five. One to change it and four to be written out because they complained about it.

Why is it that only nine out of twelve lightbulbs work in Paul McCartney's house?

Beats me. He has the same problem with his album tracks.

How many supermarket checkout girls does it take to change a lightbulb?

I don't know, I'll have to ask my supervisor.

How long does it take a Welshman to change a lightbulb?

Three hours. Five minutes to change it and two hours and fifftu-five minutes to sing a song about it.

How do wrestlers change a lightbulb?

They don't have to. It's fixed.

Why is Charles Bronson too busy to change a lightbulb?

'Cause he's out there on the street ... avenging the death of the old one.

How many Kenneth Williams's does it take to change a lightbulb?

Two. One to change it and one to talk about it on every chat show in the country.

How many Marilyn Monroes does it take to change a lightbulb?

Her light never went out.

How many hippies does it take to change a lightbulb?

Ten. One to change it and nine to pass it round.

GREAT LIGHTBULB MAN!!!
MAN! - COOL MAN - LAID BACK 'N GROOVY MAN!
COOL BULBSVILLE MAN!
HANG LOOSE MOTHER GOOSE
SWITCHED ON, MAN!

How many *News of the World* reporters does it take to change a lightbulb?

We'll never know. They all made an excuse and left.

How long does it take Nicholas Parsons to change a lightbulb?

Just a Minute.

Did Henry VIII change lightbulbs?

Sure. He was always chopping and changing.

How many shop assistants does it take to change a lightbulb?

None. They carry on chatting while *you* change it.

How do the 'That's Life' team change a lightbulb?

While making complete prats of themselves.

How many Italians does it take to change a lightbulb?

Two. An Italian woman to stand on a chair to change the bulb and an Italian man to pinch her bum while she does it.

Danny La Rue, why have you never changed that lightbulb?

'My dear boy. I've had it thirty years … isn't that right, Jack? And it's just like me. Warm, bright and never been touched by a chorus girl!'

Joan Collins … Joanie … tell us, how do you change a lightbulb?

'Often … like my lovers!'

How many *Sun* journalists does it take to change a lightbulb?

Three. That's *one* to make sure we know the bulb is naked. *One* to ask if it's gay. And *one* to consider it front page news.

How do you get Chuck Berry to change a lightbulb?

Well, first you fill a bag with two thousand dollars …

Why is it bad news to ask Teddy Kennedy to change your lightbulb?

'Cause he'll offer to drive you to the supermarket to get a new one.

Why is it bad news to ask Mark Thatcher to change a lightbulb?

You can't change a lightbulb *and* hold a compass at the same time.

How many Irishmen does it take to change a lightbulb?

Two. One to change it and one to turn the gas off at the mains just in case.

How many lighthouse keepers does it take to change a lightbulb?

Only one. But he's got to have arms thirty feet long.

How many Scotsmen does it take to change a lightbulb?

Two. One to change it and one to borrow a bulb.

How many Italians does it take to change a lightbulb?

Two. One to change it and one to persuade the old bulb to surrender.

How many Mavis Rileys does it take to change a lightbulb?

I don't knowwwwwwww.

How many Sean Penns does it take to ... ooof ... ouch ... aaghh!!!

How many Jesus Christs did it take to change a lightbulb?

The old bulb died for our sins.

How many Max Headrooms does it take to change a lightbulb?

J-j-j-j-just the one-un-un-un-un-un!

How many Irishmen does it take to change a lightbulb?

Three hundred. One to change it and the other two hundred and ninety-nine to wonder where the light went when it went out.

How did Russell Grant know it was time to change his lightbulb?

'Cause the old one went out with a big 'poof'.

How many 'Allo Allo' cast members does it take to change a lightbulb?

'Listen carefully, I will say zis only once. One!'

How many Mary Whitehouses does it take to change a lightbulb?

'I don't want to hear any four-letter words like "bulb", thank you very much!'

How many Pope John Paul I's does it take to change a lightbulb?

The old bulb died in mysterious circumstances.

How many convicts does it take to change a lightbulb?

Two. One to change it and one to ask the bulb, 'How long are you in for?'

How many Bo Dereks does it take to change a lightbulb?

10, of course.

How many composer George Harrisons does it take to change a lightbulb?

Just one because he's so fine.

How many AIDS specialists does it take to change a lightbulb?

Just the one, but remember, he's changing a lightbulb with everyone who's changed a lightbulb in the past eight years.

How do you get Marlon Brando to change a lightbulb?

Offer him a million dollars and tell him it'll only take two days.

How many Moonies does it take to change a lightbulb?

'That's an interesting point. Why don't you come back to our place and discuss it over coffee?'

How many Japanese tourists does it take to change a lightbulb?

A hundred. That's one to change it and ninety-nine to photograph the occasion.

How many double-glazing salesmen does it take to change a lightbulb?

'If you give me a minute I'll work it out on my pocket calculator and I think you'll be pleasantly surprised.'

How many Gestapo officers does it take to change a lightbulb?

'Silence! It is *we* who ask the questions!'

How many American Presidents does it take to change a lightbulb?

Two. One to change it and one to cover up for him.

KEEP WAVING MAC!
FOR GOD'S SAKE HURRY — MY ARM 'N TEETH'S HURTIN'

How many enemies of the Mafia does it take to change a lightbulb?

Who can change a lightbulb without any fingers?

How many Prince Williams does it take to change a lightbulb?

'When I am King I'll send my knights to change it!'

How many Andrew Ridgeleys does it take to change a lightbulb?

Makes no difference. He'll always be in George Michael's shadow.

How many Ken Barlows does it take to change a lightbulb?

Just the one. But while he's doing it, Mike Baldwin is bonking Deirdre.

How many Subway Vigilantes does it take to change a lightbulb?

Bang, bang, bang, bang.

How many undertakers does it take to change a lightbulb?

'The old bulb isn't dead, sir, it's in eternal rest.'

How many High Court judges does it take to change a lightbulb?

'Ahem, what is a lightbulb?'

How many Bob Dylans does it take to change a lightbulb?

The answer, my friend, is blowing in the wind.

How many Arfer Daileys does it take to change a lightbulb?

'Leave it out! 'Er indoors does all that stuff.'

How many John Waynes does it take to change a lightbulb?

Two. One to change it and one to tell the old one to get out of town by sundown.

How many Harold Wilsons does it take to change a lightbulb?

One. But it will not affect the bulb in your socket.

How many garage mechanics does it take to change a lightbulb?

'Whoo ... have you been using this bulb, then?'

How many Bernard Mannings does it take to change a lightbulb?

'There was this wog and he wanted to change a lightbulb, so he goes up to this Jewish feller ...'

How many Paul McCartneys does it take to change a lightbulb?

Just the one, but like everything else with Paul, he'll be accompanied by Linda.

How many gays does it take to change a lightbulb?

Ooh, about five. One to change it and four to criticize the shoes he's wearing.

How does a German electrician transport lightbulbs?

In a Volts-wagen.

Why won't the middle classes change a lightbulb after nine at night?

Because they always change *before* dinner.

How do they change a lightbulb in a massage parlour?

By hand.

When does a clairvoyant change a lightbulb?

About a minute before the old one blows.

Why did King Kong never change a lightbulb?

He left that to the little woman. He had her in the palm of his hand.

How many British Rail porters does it take to change a lightbulb?

Who the hell knows? I can never find one.

Why is it bad news to ask Col. Oliver North to change a lightbulb?

'Cause he'll make you believe there's nothing wrong with the lightbulb.

How many Jewish mothers does it take to change a lightbulb?

'Oy, don't worry about me, I'm fine here in the dark.'

How many Masons does it take to change a lightbulb?

Thirteen. That's one to change it and twelve to swear him to secrecy about how he did it.

If you asked a group of Masons to stand on a table and change a lightbulb, why would it take them all night?

'Cause they'd be too busy helping each other get on.

How many TUC members does it take to change a lightbulb?

'That's not my job, mate. You need an electrician.'

How does Colin Welland change a lightbulb?

With a purple face. Have you seen the size of him lately?

What do they do in Langan's Brasserie when a lightbulb blows?

If it went upstairs – nothing!

When did Mike Yarwood last change a lightbulb?

Just now, but you probably thought it was somebody else.

How does Johnny Carson change a lightbulb?

First he consults his lawyer to see how much it'll cost him in alimony if the whole thing doesn't work out.

How does Richard Attenborough change a lightbulb?

With tears in his eyes.

How does David Attenborough change a lightbulb?

First he has to be flown at licence-payer's expense to the other side of the world to be photographed knee-deep in bat guano.

How many Robert Maxwells does it take to change a lightbulb?

Two. One to run a campaign to remove the old one. And one to realize that the old one's got five more years of life at least.

How many *Private Eye* editors does it take to change a lightbulb? I think we should be told.

Ten. (That's enough editors. Ed.)

How many park keepers does it take to change a lightbulb?

Two. One to change it and the other one to say, 'You can't do that here!'

Michael Jackson, how do you change your lightbulbs?

'I don't know what you mean. All the light in my house comes from the sunbeams that live in the attic and the moonbeams on the ceiling.'

How many cobblers does it take to change a lightbulb?

Two. One to do it and one to say, 'It'll be ready on Thursday'.

How many secretaries does it take to change a lightbulb?

Two. One to forget to do it and one to blame it on 'that useless temp'.

How many Khomenei Ayatollahs does it take to change a lightbulb?

Two. One to change the bulb and one to cut the prisoner down who's hanging from the flex.

Kermit, how do you change a lightbulb?

'Oh, just like I do everything else. I can only do it if Jim Henson feels like doing it.'

How many Linda Lovelaces does it take to change a lightbulb?

69.

How many Rock Hudsons does it take to change a lightbulb?

What bum killed the old one?

How many Chelsea boutique assistants does it take to change a lightbulb?

Two. One to change it and one to measure your inside leg.

How many Woody Allens does it take to change a lightbulb?

If it's Monday Woody won't be home. He'll be playing clarinet at Michael's Pub in Greenwich Village.

How many Roger De Courceys does it take to change a lightbulb?

Don't you mean 'lightGULB'?

How many Johnny Cash's does it take to screw in a lightbulb?

'Bill or George, anything but Screw!'

How many Aussies does it take to change a lightbulb?

Thirty. One to change it and twenty-nine to crack open a few cold ones.

How many Irishmen does it take to change a lightbulb?

Five. (That's one Irishman and another and another and another and another). One to hold the bulb and the other four to turn the room round.

How many Beethovens does it take to change a lightbulb?

'You'll hef to speak up, I can't hear a vord you're sayink.'

How many Beethovens with a new hearing aid does it take to change a lightbulb?

'Half past four!'

How long does it take a feminist to change a lightbulb?

Half the time it takes a man.

How long does it take a male chauvinist to change a lightbulb?

'Change it yourself, bitch!'

How many Perry Masons does it take to change a lightbulb?

I object, Your Honour, on the grounds that the question is incompetent, irrelevant and immaterial!

How many Blockbusters contestants does it take to change a lightbulb?

Two. One to change it and one to get a cheap laugh by asking, 'May I have a P please, Bob?'

What happened when Mark Thatcher went up the ladder to change a lightbulb?

He got lost.

How many Crocodile Dundees does it take to change a lightbulb?

That's not a lightbulb! THIS is a lightbulb!

How many Bob Geldofs does it take to change a lightbulb?

'Who the … needs a lightbulb? The sun shines out of my arse!'

How many Martians does it take to change a lightbulb?

'Don't rush me, I'll do it later! I've only got two pairs of hands!'

How many doctors does it take to change a lightbulb?

'Say 99.'

How many coal delivery men does it take to change a lightbulb?

Twelve. But I was watching through the window and only counted ten.

How many Chelsea bistro waiters does it take to change a lightbulb?

Two. One to do it and one to multiply the bill.

Are you in favour of Richard Digence changing a lightbulb?

Yes, 'cause while he's changing it he's not singing one of his instantly forgettable songs.

How many rectal thermometer makers does it take to change a lightbulb?

Two. One to do it and one to tell you where to stick it!

How many Millwall supporters does it take to change a lightbulb?

Two hundred. One to do it and the rest to spray the word 'Bollocks' on the wall next to it.

How does a thermometer maker change a lightbulb?

By degrees.

How many Joan Collins's does it take to screw in a lightbulb?

Two. One to do it and one to ask, 'Is it in yet?'

How many Lord Longfords does it take to change a lightbulb?

The old one should've been released years ago. It's served its time.

How does a Jehovah's Witness change a lightbulb?

Who the hell's going to be idiot enough to let him in to find out?

Did you know Mandy Rice-Davies's boy-friend just changed a lightbulb?

Well, he would, wouldn't he?

How long does it take an Arab to change a lightbulb?

Two sheiks.

How do Salvation Army members reach up to change a lightbulb?

They stand on their heels to save soles.

How many girls from Inverness does it take to change a lightbulb?

Four and twenty. All virgins.

Why does April Ashley phone the Electricity Board every time a lightbulb blows?

She's afraid she might be cut off again.

How many Hare Krishnas does it take to change a lightbulb?

Two. One to do it and one to claim he did it in a previous life.

How many Irish firemen does it take to change a lightbulb?

Sorry, they had to go back to the fire station. They forgot the ladder.

How many Peter Pipers who picked a peck of pickled peppers does it take to change a lightbulb?

That's easy for you to say.

How many policemen does it take to change a lightbulb?

Two. One to change it and one to claim the old one fell down the stairs.

How does Dorian Gray change a lightbulb?

Agelessly.

Dionne Warwick, do you know the way to change a lightbulb?

'Wo wo wo-wo wo-wo wo wo!'

How does Kermit the Frog change a lightbulb?

On Piggyback.

OK! WHERE'S THE FROG ?
SOMEONE MENTION PIGS ?

How many *Private Eye* Editors does it take to change a lightbulb?

450 (Shurely shome mishtake).

How many Cliff Richards does it take to screw in a lightbulb?

Too late. Cliff doesn't screw anymore.

How many Brutus's does it take to change a lightbulb?

Et two.

How many Marlon Brandos does it take to change a lightbulb?

'What's my motivation?'

How many Rhett Butlers does it take to change a lightbulb?

'Frankly, my dear, I don't give a damn!'

How long does it take Monica Coghlan to change a lightbulb?

A short time. When it comes to changing lightbulbs she can knock spots off Jeffrey Archer.

When will Edgar Allan Poe change a lightbulb?

Nevermore!

Can Rambo change a lightbulb?

Yes. No law, no war, no man can stop him.

Dr Ruth, how big a lightbulb should be put in a light socket?

'Size is not important.'

Lady Chatterley, can you change a lightbulb?

'Not tonight, I've got a head gardener!'

How does Jerry Lewis change a lightbulb in France?

While walking on water.

What does Stanley Kubrick say as he changes a lightbulb?

'Take 46! Action!'

How do you change a lightbulb at Cynthia Payne's house?

With a lightbulb voucher.

How does Pia Zadora change a lightbulb?

Financed by her husband ... but it'll just be another disaster.

How often did Edmund Halley change a lightbulb?

Every seventy-five years.

How many Sir Ralph Halperns does it take to change a lightbulb?

Just one, but he'll do it five times a night.

How does Goldilocks change a lightbulb?

With a bear behind.

What's the Eddie Waring method of screwing in a lightbulb?
    Up and under.

Why did Gary Cooper always change his own lightbulbs?
    Because a man's gotta do what a man's gotta do.

What does Colonel Sanders do after changing a lightbulb?
    Licks his fingers.

How should Arthur Scargill change a lightbulb?
    With his feet in a bucket of water.

How does Eric Morley change three lightbulbs?

In reverse order.

How many British tourists in Marbella does it take to change a lightbulb?

Too late, the Germans got there first.

How often did The Goons change a lightbulb?

Only in the mating season.

How many Selina Scotts does it take to change a lightbulb?

Just the one, but she's out at the moment at her Keep Thick class.

How does Hughie Green change a lightbulb?

Most sincerely.

How many Batmans and Robins does it take to change a lightbulb?

'Holy filament, Batman! Does this mean the end of the lightbulb? Tune in next week and find out!'

How did Oliver Twist change a lightbulb?

How the Dickens should I know?

How many Reginald Perrin's bosses does it take to change a lightbulb?

'I didn't get where I am today by changing lightbulbs!'

What did Davy Crockett say when General Santa Anna told him to change the lightbulb at the Alamo?

'You're *telling* me to do it? You and whose army?'

Why do people over in Africa, India and Australia never worry about the dark when their lightbulbs blow?

'Cause the sun never sets on the British Empire.

How many James Burkes does it take to change a lightbulb?

One. But you'll never be able to understand how he did it.

Why does it take Norman Bates so long to change a lightbulb?

'Cause he has to ask his mother first.

If his lightbulb blows, why does Gene Kelly do a handstand in the middle of the room?

'Cause he's still light on his feet.

What did Florence Nightingale do when her lamp blew out?

Called the Light Brigade.

How many Arthur C. Clarkes does it take to change a lightbulb?

2001 ... 2002 ... 2003

How many sado-masochists does it take to change a lightbulb?

Beats the hell out of me!

How many American tourists does it take to change a lightbulb?

Six. One to change it and five to complain that they haven't had a decent cup of coffee since they left home.

What does Art Garfunkel do when his lightbulb blows?

Just what he does all the time. Calls up Paul Simon to organize another reunion concert.

How does Mr Kipling change a lightbulb?

He doesn't. He's too busy making exceedingly small cakes.

How can you recognize Elton John's lightbulb flex?

It swings both ways.

How many Daleks does it take to change a lightbulb?

Extermin-eight!

How does Victor Sylvester change five lightbulbs?

Slow, slow, quick-quick, slow.

Judy Carne, is that a lightbulb plug?

'It may be a plug to you but it's a socket to me!' (SPLASH)

How many models-turned-actresses does it take to change a lightbulb?

Just the one, but she really wants to direct.

How many jock strap collectors does it take to change a lightbulb?

Just the one, but he needs your support.

How many British tourists does it take to change a lightbulb?

Ten. That's one to change it and nine to write to 'That's Life' to complain about it.

How many Robin Days does it take to change a lightbulb?

'The Robin Day in the third row ... No, not you ... the Robin Day in the glasses ... No, not you either ... the Robin Day in the spotted bowtie ... No, not you ... the Robin Day in the pinstripe suit ... Yes, you, sir ... What's your question?'

'How many Robin Days does it take to change a lightbulb?'

'Sorry, we seem to have run out of time!'

How many Ronald Reagans does it take to change a lightbulb?

'I don't remember!'

How many Bruce Forsyths does it take to change a lightbulb?

Just the one. You don't get anything for a pair.

How many traffic wardens does it take to change a lightbulb?

Three. One to change it, one to clamp it and one to make a note of its patent number.

How did Sarah Brightman get to change her first major lightbulb?

First, she had to marry Andrew Lloyd Webber ...

How many barbers does it take to change a lightbulb?

Two. One to change it and one to ask, 'What about something for the weekend, sir?'

How many Post Office clerks does it take to change a lightbulb?

'You'll have to ask at the next window. I'm going to lunch.'

How does a hooker change a lightbulb?

That depends how you want her to change it, darling.

How does Victoria Principal change a lightbulb?

She takes off all her clothes then ten years later she says she was forced into it.

How many Sloane Rangers does it take to screw in a lightbulb?

None. Sloane Rangers screw in the back of Range Rovers.

How many Michael Ciminos does it take to change a lightbulb?

One. The bulb cost 30p but by the time he's finished changing it it'll cost five times that much.

How many 'Eastenders' producers does it take to change a lightbulb?

Three. One to change it on Tuesday, one to change it on Thursday and one to change them both again on Sunday.

How many Michael Jacksons does it take to change a lightbulb?

If you'd kept the old bulb in an oxygen chamber it'd have lived for ever.

How many Angela Lansburys does it take to change a lightbulb?

The old bulb was still alive till she got here.

What number of British Telecom operators does it take to change a lightbulb?

One. Sorry, wrong number!

How many L. Ron Hubbards does it take to change a lightbulb?

Nobody believes the old one to be dead.

How many Victor Kiams does it take to change a lightbulb?

He liked the bulb so much he bought the Central Electricity Generating Board ... and went on TV to brag about it.

How many Lynn Faulds-Woods does it take to change a lightbulb?

Two. One to show you how to do it and one to cut her hand on the broken glass.

How many Dukes of Hazzard does it take to change a lightbulb?

Four. Two to change it and two to climb out through the windows.

How many Syd Lawrences does it take to change a lightbulb?

A-one, a-two, a-three, a-four!

How many Patsy Kensits does it take to change a lightbulb?

Well, as she can't act and can't sing, what makes you think she can change a lightbulb?

How many David Souls does it take to change a lightbulb?

Sorry, David's not here. He's gone to a wife-beating party.

How did Rowan Atkinson put out a thousand lightbulbs at one time?

He opened his one-man show on Broadway ... then closed it.

Pussycat, can you change a lightbulb?
'Me? 'Ow?'

Sylvester Stallone, how do you change a lightbulb?
'With my bare hands ... okay?'

Arnold Schwarzenegger, how do you change a lightbulb?

'With my bare *teeth*!'

'Er … Mr Stallone, Mr Schwarzenegger says he can change a lightbulb with his bare teeth!'

'Uh … Say, what kind of name is Schwarzenegger for an *American*?'

How does Murray Walker change a lightbulb?

With *THE* em*PHA*sis on the wr*ONG* sy*L-LAB*le at the *TOP* of *HIS* voice!

How does Kathleen Turner change a lightbulb?

Who cares? What I really want to know is her phone number!

How does Mr Spock change a lightbulb?
Logically.

Why can't Scotty change a lightbulb right now?
Ye canny change the laws of lightbulbs!

What does Mr Spock say when a lightbulb blows?
'It's dead, Jim!'

Can a hedgehog crossing the M1 change a lightbulb?
No and that's flat!

Does Ian Paisley change lightbulbs?
Is the Pope a Catholic?

'Waiter, there's a lightbulb in my soup.'
'Sorry, sir, we've run out of flies!'

How many horny monks does it take to change a lightbulb?
Nun!

How many nuns does it take to change a lightbulb?
Dunno, they're all over at the monastery with those horny monks.

How many comic strip artists does it take to change a lightbulb?

Would that be the lightbulb that goes on over his head?

How does John Hurt change a lightbulb?

First he arrives at the studio at 6.00 a.m. and undergoes a five-hour makeup job ...

Who changes the lightbulbs at Buckingham Palace?

'My husband and I.'

How many nightclub bouncers does it take to change a lightbulb?

'What sort of a ----- question is that? Are you looking for trouble, son? 'Ere, you was in here last week, wasn't you?'

How many Alvin Stardusts does it take to change a lightbulb?

First things first. He has to change his name again and that takes priority.

How many Joan Crawfords does it take to change a lightbulb?

Two. One to change it and one to beat the crap out of it with a wire coat hanger.

How many dustmen does it take to change a lightbulb?

Two. One to change it and one to drop the old one on the front path.

Does an anorexic need to change a lightbulb?

No, she's light enough.

How does Jimmy Young change a lightbulb?

Like he does his TV show. When no one's watching.

George Burns, how do you change a lightbulb?

'Lemme tell you something, son. I'm ninety-one years old. I work Vegas three months of the year. I'm planning two TV Specials. I'm writing another book. I'm in the middle of another Oh God movie and I smoke six Havana cigars every day! Who's got *time* to change a lightbulb?'

'**M**adonna, how do you change a lightbulb?'

'In my undies ... in case someone is filming me while I do it!'

How many Sylvester Stallones does it take to change a lightbulb?

Two. One to change it and one to insist his brother Frank writes the music.

How many Donald McGills does it take to change a lightbulb?

One. But he has to stand on a fat lady's boobs to reach it.

How many Roy Rogers's does it take to change a lightbulb?

Just the one, but first he'd like to sing a song and then he'll have the dead one stuffed and mounted.

How many Elvis Presleys does it take … too late, he's eaten it.

How many Ozzy Osbournes does it take to change a lightbulb?

'Who needs light? Bats only come out in the dark and I'm hungry!'

How many Blue Peter presenters does it take to change a lightbulb?

Two. One to demonstrate how it's done and one to show a lightbulb that was changed earlier.

How many teachers does it take to change a lightbulb?

Put your hand up if you know the answer.

What was the snotty Jack the Ripper's reaction when a strange woman asked him to change a lightbulb?

He cut her dead.

Does Anne Diamond change lightbulbs?

Yes, but you'll have to get up early to catch her.

How does Timmy Mallett change a lightbulb?

Wimpishly.

You know, I'm bored with watching schizophrenics change lightbulbs.

Well, when you've seen two you've seen 'em all.

What does Alan Freeman say to the lightbulb after he changes it?

'All right. Stay bright!'

What is Captain Kirk's reaction when you ask him to change a lightbulb?

He tells you to boldly go to Hell!

Why did Sir Edmund Hillary change a lightbulb?

Because it was there!

Why don't we know how long it takes Janet Street-Porter to change a lightbulb?

Because her face can stop the clock.

Why can't Ian Botham change a lightbulb?

Because he's gone to pot.

How long does it take to change a lightbulb in Woody Allen's house?

A Mia minute.

When does a British publican know the lightbulb he just changed is okay?

When it gets warmer than the beer.

Why didn't Dorothy Parker change lightbulbs?

Too f---ing busy and vice versa.

How does Christopher Lee change a lightbulb?

'Look! Let's get something straight! I haven't made a horror movie for more than twenty years! I'm accepted as a serious actor! And stop laughing!'

'**F**rank Sinatra, how do you change a lightbulb?'

'Who let the goddamn press in here anyway?'

'**M**r President, how do you change a lightbulb?'

'Well ... you know ... if that little old lightbulb is the same age as me, maybe he's a mite too old to change!'

How many estate agents does it take to change a lightbulb?

Two. One to get you interested in changing it and another to walk in and point out five other people interested in the same lightbulb. 'Perhaps if you paid us a deposit ...?'

What's the Edward Woodward method of changing lightbulbs?

He makes sure everyone gets lightbulbs equally.

When did Callan change a lightbulb?

When he was feeling Lonely!